A Child's Book
of Blessings and Prayers

A Child's Book of Blessings and Prayers

Collected by Eliza Blanchard

Illustrated by Rocco Baviera

Printed in the United States

Illustrations by Rocco Baviera

ISBN 1-55896-535-1 / 978-1-55896-535-5

10 09 08 / 6 5 4 3 2 1

Library of Congress Cataloging-in-Publication Data

A child's book of blessings and prayers / edited by Eliza Blanchard.
    p. cm.
 ISBN-13: 978-1-55896-535-5 (pbk. : alk. paper)
 ISBN-10: 1-55896-535-1 (pbk. : alk. paper) 1. Children—Prayers and devotions. I. Blanchard, Eliza, 1950-

BV265.C465 2008
242'.82—dc22

2007038042

We gratefully acknowledge permission to reprint the following copyrighted material: prayer by Meg Barnhouse from "Night Prayers," *Waking Up the Karma Fairy*, reprinted with permission of the author; prayer by Sirona Knight, from *Goddess Bless!*, reprinted with permission of the author; Rumi prayer translated by Coleman Barks, reprinted with permission of Coleman Barks; translation of *Rig Veda* reprinted with permission of The World Prayers Project, www.worldprayers.org; prayer by Nathan Segal, copyright © Nathan Segal 1969, 2007, reprinted with permission of the author; prayer by Gary Kowalski, from *Green Mountain Spring and Other Leaps of Faith*, reprinted with permission of the author; prayer by Rebecca Parker reprinted with permission of the author.

Dear Reader,

Like prayers and blessings everywhere, the prayers in
this book speak words of joy, thanksgiving, hope, and
sadness. People of different religions all over the world
created them. Some of these words are old—so old that
we will never know who first wrote them or spoke the
words out loud. Some are written by people living today.

Do you want to pray? Many things that happen in our
lives bring us to pray: a birthday, bedtime, a holiday
celebration, a friend moving away. Prayers can express so
many feelings! You can pray out loud or to yourself. If
you try, you will find a prayer that feels right to you.

Blessings,

Eliza Blanchard

There is a love
Holding me.
There is a love
Holding you.
There is a love
Holding all.
I rest
in this love.

—Rebecca Parker,
Unitarian Universalist

1

Where I sit is holy,
Holy is the ground.
Forest, mountain, river
Listen to the sound.
Great Spirit circle
All around me.

—*Blackfoot chant*

2

God made the sun
God made the trees
God made the mountains
and God made me!

Thank you for the sun
Thank you for the trees
Thank you for the mountains
and thank you for me!

—*Anonymous*

3

May all the beings
in all the worlds be happy.
May all the beings
in all the worlds be happy.
May all the beings
in all the worlds be happy.
Om Peace, Peace, Peace.

—*Rig Veda, Hindu*

4

Grandfather, Great Spirit, fill us with the light.
Give us strength to understand and eyes to see.
Teach us to walk the soft earth as relatives to all that live.

—*Sioux prayer*

May all I say and all I think
Be in harmony with thee.
God within me, God beyond me,
Maker of the trees.

—*Chinook Psalter*

6

I sing to the Mother Gaia.
I sing to the Father Sun.
I sing to the living in the garden where
the Mother and the Father are one.

—*Pagan chant*

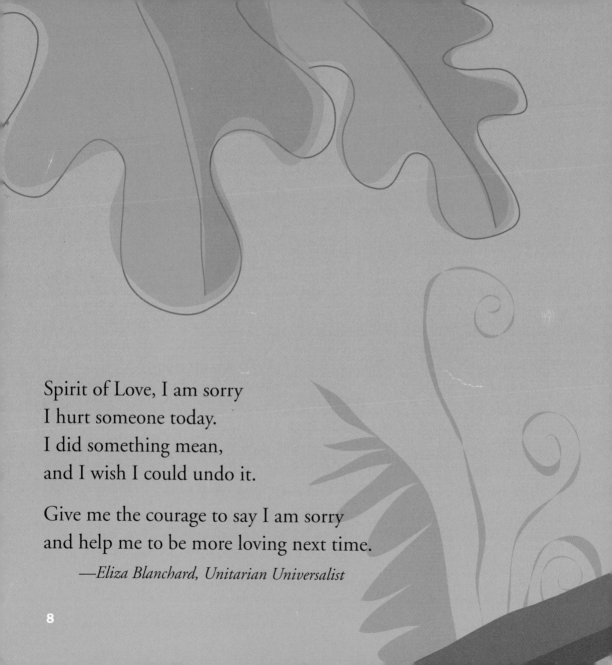

Spirit of Love, I am sorry
I hurt someone today.
I did something mean,
and I wish I could undo it.

Give me the courage to say I am sorry
and help me to be more loving next time.

—*Eliza Blanchard, Unitarian Universalist*

I thank you, Lord, for knowing me
better than I know myself,
and for letting me know myself
better than others know me.
Make me, I ask you then,
better than they suppose.
And forgive me for what they do not know.

—*Islamic prayer*

Be who you are
and may you be blessed
in all that you are.

—*Jewish blessing*

On your birthday we pray
Green be the grass you walk on,
Blue be the skies above you,
Pure be the joys that surround you,
True be the hearts that love you.

—*Irish blessing*

Earth, who gives to us this food,
Sun, who makes it ripe and good,
Dear Earth, dear Sun, by you we live.
To you our loving thanks we give.

—*Anonymous*

Thank you for the world so sweet
Thank you for the food we eat
Thank you for the birds that sing
Thank you, God, for everything

—*Christian prayer*

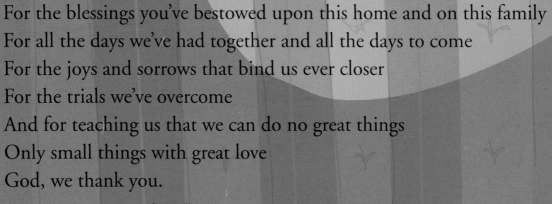

For the blessings you've bestowed upon this home and on this family
For all the days we've had together and all the days to come
For the joys and sorrows that bind us ever closer
For the trials we've overcome
And for teaching us that we can do no great things
Only small things with great love
God, we thank you.

—*Anonymous (adapted)*

Do all the good you can,
In all the ways you can,
To all the people you can,
At all the times you can,
As long as ever you can.

—*R. Monckton Milnes,*
Christian

Dear God,
Thank you for my friend next door
And my friend across the street
And please help me to be a friend
To each and every one I meet.
Amen

—*Anonymous*

Dear God,
May I be kind,
Strong and brave,
Joyful, useful, loving,
Honest and healthy.

—Meg Barnhouse,
Unitarian Universalist

17

Spirit of Life, make us truly thankful
for these and all other blessings.
Amen

—*Christian grace (adapted)*

From you I receive,
To you I give.
Together we share,
And by this we live.

—*Nathan Segal, Jewish*

19

For all we eat, and all we wear,
For daily bread, and nightly care,
We thank you, Spirit of Life.
Amen

—Christian grace (adapted)

Goddess, bless this food you have given me.
Let it be filled with your divine energy
So that I will be healthy
And live a long and happy life.
Goddess bless! Blessed be!

—*Sirona Knight, Pagan*

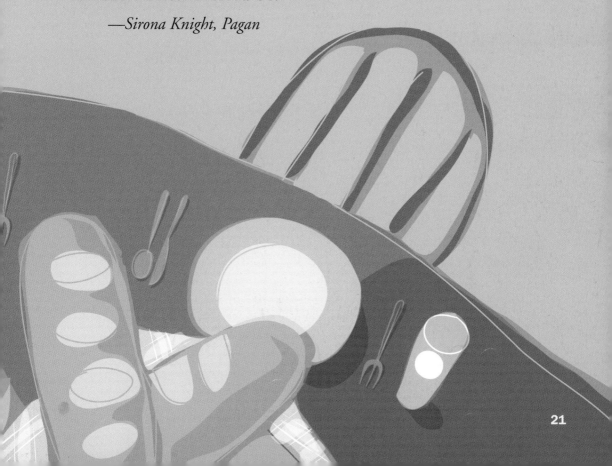

Loving Spirit,
Be our guest,
Dine with us,
Share our bread,
That our table
Might be blessed
And our souls be fed.

—*Gary Kowalski,*
Unitarian Universalist

22

Bless this house which is our home.
May we welcome all who come.

—*Anonymous*

Let us bless the source of life
that brings forth bread from the earth.
—*Jewish blessing*

For food in a world where many walk in hunger
For faith in a world where many walk in fear
For friends in a world where many walk alone
We give you thanks, O God.
Amen

—*Anonymous (adapted)*

I think over again my small adventures, my fears,
These small ones that seemed so big,
All the vital things I had to get and to reach.
And yet there is only one great thing,
The only thing.
To live to see the great day that dawns
And the light that fills the world.

  —Inuit song

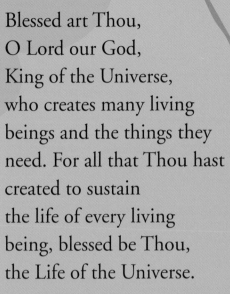

Blessed art Thou,
O Lord our God,
King of the Universe,
who creates many living
beings and the things they
need. For all that Thou hast
created to sustain
the life of every living
being, blessed be Thou,
the Life of the Universe.

—*Jewish grace*

At night, I open the window
and ask the moon to come
and press its face into mine.
Breathe into me.
Close the word-door,
and open the love-window.

The moon won't use the door,
only the window.

—Jelaluddin Rumi, Muslim

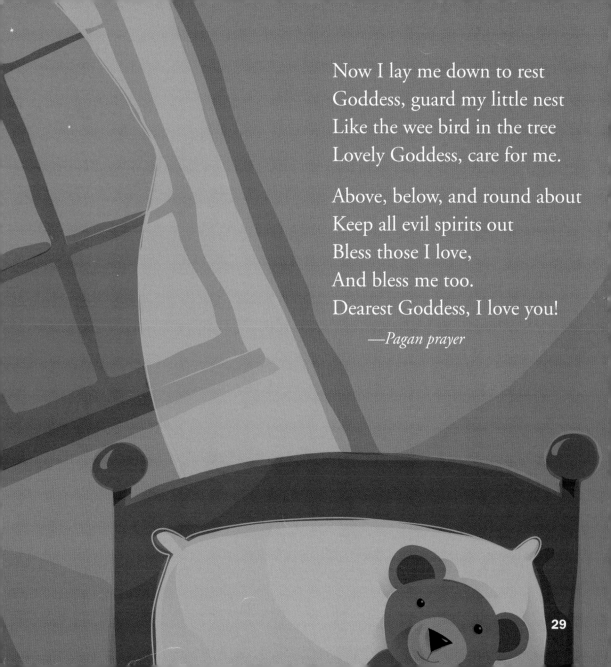

Now I lay me down to rest
Goddess, guard my little nest
Like the wee bird in the tree
Lovely Goddess, care for me.

Above, below, and round about
Keep all evil spirits out
Bless those I love,
And bless me too.
Dearest Goddess, I love you!

—*Pagan prayer*

Day is done
Gone the sun
From the lake,
From the hills,
From the sky.
All is well, safely rest.
God is nigh.

—Anonymous

For Young Readers

Aisha's Moonlit Walk: Stories and Celebrations for the Pagan Year by Anika Stafford. Skinner House, 2005.

Because Nothing Looks Like God by Lawrence and Karen Kushner. Jewish Lights, 2000.

Blackfoot by Mary A. Stout. Gareth Stevens, 2005.

Can I Pray with My Eyes Open? by Susan Taylor Brown. Hyperion, 1999.

Chinook Indians by Suzanne Morgan Williams. Heinemann, 2003.

Dear God: Children's Letters to God by David Heller. Perigee, 1994.

God Lives in Glass: Reflections of God Through the Eyes of Children by Robert J. Landy. Skylight Paths, 2001.

God's Paintbrush by Sandy Eisenberg Sasso. Jewish Lights, 2004.

Hide-and-Seek with God: A Collection of Stories for Children by Mary Ann Moore. Skinner House, 2005.

How Does God Listen? by Kay Lindahl and Cindy Maloney. Skylight Paths, 2005.

How People Worship by Julie and Robert Brown. Gareth Stevens, 1992.

Ituko: An Inuit Child by Francois Goalec. Blackbirch, 2005.

Many Ways: How Families Practice Their Beliefs and Religions by Shelley Rotner and Sheila Kelly. Millbrook, 2003.

Sioux by D.L. Birchfield. Gareth Stevens, 2002.

The Story of Religion by Betsy Maestro. Clarion, 1996.

This Is My Faith: Christianity by Anita Ganeri. Barron's Educational Series, 2006.

This Is My Faith: Hinduism by Holly Wallace. Barron's Educational Series, 2006.

This Is My Faith: Islam by Anita Ganeri. Barron's Educational Series, 2006.

This Is My Faith: Judaism by Anita Ganeri. Barron's Educational Series, 2006.

Unitarian Universalism Is a Really Long Name by Jennifer Dant. Skinner House, 2006.

What Is God? by Etan Boritzer. Firefly, 1990.

Where Does God Live? by August Gold and Matthew J. Perlman. Skylight Paths, 2001.

For Parents

The Book of New Family Traditions: How to Create Great Rituals for Holidays and Everyday by Meg Cox. Running Press, 2003.

The Gift of Faith: Tending the Spiritual Lives of Children by Jeanne Harrison Nieuwejaar. Skinner House, 2003.

How to Bury a Goldfish and Other Ceremonies and Celebrations for Everyday Life by Louise Nayer and Virginia Lang. Skinner House, 2007.